UNEVEN STEVEN

KENNETH POBO

ASSURE PRESS

Copyright © 2020 by Kenneth Pobo.

All Rights Reserved. No part of this book may be performed, recorded, used or reproduced in any manner whatsoever without the written consent of the author and the permission of the publisher except in the case of brief quotations embodied in critical articles and review.

ASSURE PRESS

An imprint of Assure Press Publishing & Consulting, LLC

www.assurepress.org

Publisher's Note: Assure Press books may be purchased for educational, business, or sales promotional use. For information, please visit the website.

Uneven Steven/ Kenneth Pobo — 1st ed.

ISBN-13: 978-1-7335897-6-5
Library of Congress Control Number: 2020936575
eISBN-13: 978-1-7335897-7-2

CONTENTS

Acknowledgments	vii

A QUIET KID

TWENTY YEARS LATER	3
STEVE WAS THE BOY	4
STEVE IN FIFTH GRADE	6
WATER TOWER	7
WHAT KIND OF A HERO	8
STEVE'S MOTHER	10
A SHEET OF PAPER	11
A QUIET KID	12
STEVE IN BROAD AND NARROW DAYLIGHT	14
STEVE IN THE SPRING	15
JUNIOR YEAR SEX ED	16
STEVE'S TERRIBLE YELLOW SHIRT	17
RUDY TOLD STEVE	18
STEVE AT 13	19
STEVE'S FIRST CRUSH	20
HYMNS	21
HIGH-SCHOOL TERM PAPER	22
STEVE BURNING	23
STEVE'S SECRETS	24
OUT FROM UNDER	25
THE BARGAIN	26
A GRIEF	27
TRACING PAPER	28
STUDIO APARTMENT	29
STEVE'S FOREIGN LANGUAGE	30
STORY OF A GARDEN	31
BY HAND	33

EMPTY TREE

AFRAID TO TELL	37
STEVE STEW	38
STEVE'S FRIDGE LOOKED INTO	39

STEVE COMPLEX	40
BROWN CORDS	41
LEFT-HANDED MONKEY WRENCH	42
SNAPSHOT	43
SMILE	44
STEVE'S LOBSTERS	45
I-95	47
REALLY?	48
OVERHEARD	50
ODORS FROM OTHER WINDOWS	51
SWIMMER STEVE	52
STEVE AFTER JOGGING	53
STEVE OUT FOR A WALK	54
STEVE AND THE EMPTY TREE	55
STEVE BARKING AT THE MOON	56
STEVE PAINTING	57
STEVE READY	58
STEVE READS HUCK FINN	59
STEVE STARRING IN BERGMAN'S Cries and Whispers	60
WHAT STEVE DID ON HIS SUMMER VACATION	61
DRY SPELL	62
THE JOKE	63
TURBULENCE	64

LATELY

STEVE THIS MORNING	67
MORNING COFFEE AND EVENING STENCH	68
STEVE AND THE BURGLAR	70
STEVE IN PURGATORY	71
STEVE IN PARADISE	72
STEVE DISAPPEARING	73
STEVE CUTS	74
STEVE AND CHILDREN	75
STEVE IN THE ORCHARD	76
EARLY	77
AFRICAN VIOLET STEVE	78
STEVE LOOKS AT CLOUDS	79
THE NIGHT HAS 1007 EYES	80
DOLLY PARTON	82
STEVE'S OPEN FLOWER	83

BLUE TRAIN	84
STEVE'S FLASHLIGHT	85
STEVE FLICKERS	86
STEVE LATELY	87
About the Author	89
Also by Kenneth Pobo	91

ACKNOWLEDGMENTS

I would like to thank the editors of the following journals for publishing work from this collection:

"Twenty Years Later" *No Exit*
"Steve Was the Boy" *The Outrider*
"Steve in Fifth Grade" *Cantaraville*
"Water Tower" *Liberty Hill Review*
"What Kind of Hero" *Hawaii Pacific Review*
"Steve's Mother" *Facets*
"A Sheet of Paper" *The Listening Eye*
"A Quiet Kid" *Owen Wister Review*
"Steve in the Spring" *Turbulence*
"Steve at 13" *The Gay Review* (Canada)
"Steve's Terrible Yellow Shirt" *Folio*
"Rudy Told Me" *Concrete Wolf*
"Junior High Sex Ed" *Algebra of Owls* (England)
"Steve's First Crush" *Armarolla*
"Hymns" *Cantaraville*
"High-School Term Paper" *Tipton Poetry Review*
"Steve Burning" *The Catylizer Review*
"Steve's Secrets" *Leapings*
"Out From Under" *Montana Mouthful*
"The Bargain" *Forage*
"A Grief" *The Poet's Cut*
"Tracing Paper" *Comrades*
"Studio Apartment" *Cape Rock*
"Steve's Foreign Language" *Mudfish*
"Story of a Garden" *JAW Magazine*
"By Hand" *Snake River Review*
"Afraid to Tell" *Iota* (England)
"Steve Stew" *Prairie Winds*
"Steve's Fridge Looked Into" *Ibbetson Street Press*

"Steve Complex" *Matador Review*
"Left-Handed Monkey Wrench" *Haight-Asbury Literary Review*
"Smile" *King Log*
"Steve's Lobsters" *Forpoetry.com*
"I-95" *Caught In The Net* (England)
"Really?" *Panic: Poetry Brixton* (England)
"Swimmer Steve" *Tenderness, Yeah*
"Steve After Jogging" *WTF Magazine*
"Steve Out for a Walk" *American Writing*
"Odors from Other Windows" *The Plowman* (Canada)
"Overheard" *Bottom of the World* (England)
"Steve and the Empty Tree" *Black River Review*
"Steve Barking at the Moon" *Forpoetry.com*
"Steve Painting" *Alchemy*
"Steve Ready" *Red Coral*
"Steve Reads *Huck Finn*" *Galleys*
"Steve Starring in Bergman's Cries And Whispers" *The Recussant*
"What Steve Did on His Summer Vacation" *Mojave River Review*
"Dry Spell" *Canadian Dimension* (Canada)
"The Joke" *Chiron Review*
"Turbulence" *Philadelphia Poets*
"This Morning" *West Trade Review*
"Morning Coffee And Evening Stench" *Full of Crow, Something To Be Said* (chapbook)
"Steve in Purgatory" *Double Entendre*
"Steve in Paradise" *Shrike*
"Steve Disappearing" *Double Entendre*
"Steve Cuts" *Hidden Oak Review*
"Steve and Children" *dig* (Canada)
"Steve in the Orchard" *Excursus*
"Early" *Cherry Blossom Review*
"African Violet Steve" *ArLiJo (Arlington Literary Journal)*
"Steve Looks at Clouds" *Spoon River Quarterly*
"The Night Has 1007 Eyes" *Caper Journal*

"Dolly Parton" *Matador Review*
"Steve's Open Flower" *Farmer's Market*
"Blue Train" *Ithacalit.com*
"Steve's Flashlight" *Verse-Virtual*
"Steve Flickers" *Lavender Wolves*
"Steve Lately" *Pivot*

UNEVEN STEVEN

A QUIET KID

TWENTY YEARS LATER

six-year-old steve
plays dress-ups
with marcy who lives
two houses behind his

steve's mom says she
must put a stop to
this makes him go home

twenty years
later he remembers
fondly turning a sheet
into a formal he looks
at the suit he wears
to work too tight
colorless in his living

room he steps out of it
stuffs it in a silver bucket
douses it with charcoal
lighter fluid drops
a lit match dances
hoots and sings
naked off-key

STEVE WAS THE BOY

who in fourth grade
played Chinese jump rope
with the girls at recess
and cut out paper dolls at home.

While walking to school, Billy
caught up to him and said that
Steve wasn't a real boy.
His mom called Steve
a half and half,
and she should know since
she ran the Washington School

Fall Fair. She added that Steve
would grow up to play the girl
on dates, maybe wear dresses
and pretty hats--Billy
should be nice to Steve,
who couldn't help it. He had
to treat Penny well
in the Special Ed. class. She was
almost blind. And Richie
had his left leg cut off
below the knee. Steve

wondered which half was the boy?
Which the girl?
His parents put half and half
in their coffee. Being two people
in one—

how to grow them both,
and if you did would the others
leave you alone?

STEVE IN FIFTH GRADE

Mrs. Wood tells Steve's parents
that her students perch
on their seats, feels she's in

an aviary--kids ready to fly
where she can't see them.
His mom says they watch him
climb trees, as if he's trying to rise
over the house. Home again,

they find him perched in the elm.
He says he'll stay all night. Hungry,
he comes down for supper,
thinks school and home

are traps, has no choice
but to fly into both.

WATER TOWER

At twelve Steve fears his bones
redrawing the map of his skin,

climbs most anything
to get high enough above touch
football and algebra, the risk
of falling sweetening each stretch.

On a wet August afternoon
while climbing
the water tower
sneakers slip,
his fall broken
by multi-colored glads
"in memory of Emma Houghton."

A broken leg. By October
he's climbing toward shooting stars--

police flashlights beam up,
his steps more nimble.

WHAT KIND OF A HERO

for a kid like me?
A football player?
A general?
I hate football,
don't want to kill anybody
except playground
bullies who taunt

the sissy
who carries books
like a girl,
throws *like a girl*
and walks *like a girl.*
I figure they hate girls
but will marry them
someday, hearts given
to quarterbacks

and soldiers. I don't
hate girls, love Chinese
jump rope and playing
house. My friend Marcy
and I pretend we live

inside a marigold,
airplane bees overhead.
Dad says to leave
the marigold

and *act like a man,*

a tough act--it gets you
a job at 25,
a heart attack at 50.

STEVE'S MOTHER

My mother went to divorce court,
cited for alienation
of affection. She explored more
than a few loves, got no support
from any I remember. One
she loved, a movie-handsome bore.
I wanted to see her happy--
they flopped. Mother couldn't get free

of leeches, parasites, and knots.
Local gossip went round and round.
I kept out of sight, fed our pets,
did my homework, scrubbed pans and pots.
Claiming not to be lost or found,
she fed park pigeons her secrets.

A SHEET OF PAPER

Mr. Janko, the gym
teacher, gets a phone
call, goes into
the locker room
while the boys circle
Steve, call him *queer*,
faggot, *cocksucker*,
asshole. Flattened,
a sneaker pressed
into his side, spit
on his arm, Steve
thinks soon I'll be
a piece of paper
floating higher
than words, landing
on the school roof.
If it snows, I
won't care--a paper,
I'm blank. Winter
will write a love letter
on me, words to clutch
the next time they
try to wipe out words
they fear, choosing
teams to make sure
someone loses.

A QUIET KID

Steve is such a quiet kid,
neighborhood parents agree,
never starts a fight, always
polite, always reading.
They don't know he feels

a train speeding at him,
motionless on the tracks,
the train less real than boys
who press jagged glass
words into him at school
where he gets B's,
is a loner who walks
too fast down the hall
to get to his locker
and out of the high
school before others

follow after. He knows
don't talk back, just take it:
talk back and they multiply,
never leave you alone.

At home you're smiling
when mom asks about
your day. You go into
your room and read
about snakes, can't shed
the one skin you have,

but it can be ripped off,
nobody noticing.

STEVE IN BROAD AND NARROW DAYLIGHT

Steve: a bow tie and white
shirt. Mrs. Craig
insists Viet Nam

is God's
will and Jesus loves
us--leaving that

behind was grief,
relief. Now he seeks
butterfly

launching pads,
opens a window,
flexes and breaks

from a dahlia's
pink, new
colors calling.

STEVE IN THE SPRING

of 1967 he sang Ronnie Dove's
"My Babe" while riding his bike,
unaware that in 5 short months

bullies would come after him
daily. Physical fitness,
mental torture. He never knew
what he did to cause it. Probably nothing--

surely by now these kids have changed.
He pictures them like Jonathan Edwards
pictured sinners in God's hands,
dangled over fire—

he starts humming "My Babe" again
looking over his shoulder.

JUNIOR YEAR SEX ED

The gym teacher deflates
mystery like a bike tire,
welcomes questions, well,
some questions. Little

applies to me. What about
gay sex, gay love?

Ask anything
and it's my head
bashed against a locker.
Health Class.
Not my health--

a roomful of boys,
some of us standing behind
a door, shaking the handle,
the lock firm.

STEVE'S TERRIBLE YELLOW SHIRT

In junior high, I wore
a terrible yellow shirt--
plate patterns spread
from back to stomach,
something to live down
years later over yearbook
cocktail chatter.

Lawrence Welk conducted
in our house to my father's
tapping foot, Budweiser
in his hand, my mother
writing Bible lessons.

With a black transistor
radio, I waited
for Capsule Countdown
on WCFL, Chicago's top ten
reasons to live,

sank cash into roses,
planted them in front
of our white house

in Villa Park, Illinois,
a town frozen in 1939.
I hadn't said dirty words yet.
Asters turned blue
flashlights on our street.

RUDY TOLD STEVE

In Sunday School
during junior high,
Rudy often got swatted
for talking or for doodling
on his church bulletin.

While we worked on
Plaster of Paris crosses,
he told me how
to masturbate.
I didn't believe him

but tried it in the john.
It worked! When I told him
he said sometimes *The Song
of Solomon* got him hard.
That didn't work for me.

Thinking of Rudy worked great.
I never let him know.
By high school he quit
church. For years I heard

hate sermons, wanked at home
over hot guys in the pews.

STEVE AT 13

Dad's at work and mom's at church, so Dale and I dance to Lou Christie's "Self Expression." After playing it five times, we roll cigarettes out of paper towels and elm leaves. Smoke coming out his nose makes Dale look like a dragon. I'm scared my folks'll smell it when they return. We dance some more to Tommy James and his favorite Pet Clark. At 4:30, he has to leave or he'll never get home by five. When he turns to go, I realize I'd love to kiss him, but say we'll talk on the phone later, watch his Schwinn racer, light blue jacket, auburn hair. Sick to my stomach, damp, happy, I hear mom come in the back door.

STEVE'S FIRST CRUSH

In an under-construction house,
Steve and Dale jump into the cool
dark of what will be a basement.
Hands begin to roam. Pants come off.
It's dangerous.

Workmen can return. Others
might catch them, yet
they don't stop.

Dale attends Bereans,
a church group "who searched
the scriptures daily." He searches
record stores for The Supremes
and Pet Clark. Steve loves Tommy
James and the Shondells—

they fight about it. Choose.
Either Pet or Tommy.
They stop going
to the unfinished house. Dale
takes up with Ron:
Strip Monopoly. Steve pictures
nudity in Marvin Gardens,
hopes he'll grow out of basements
and boys.

The basements only get deeper—
even still, he takes the leap.

HYMNS

In church, he'd sing so quietly,
only made a joyful noise when
he got home and his parents went
outside to garden or wash the car.
He sang loud, clear,
and off-key. His parents stomped in,
shouted TURN THAT DOWN.

He did--his own songs of praise,
put back in a box holding tight shoes
at the bottom of the closet.

HIGH-SCHOOL TERM PAPER

I wrote mine about Thomas Hardy.
He's depressing. That's why I chose him.
People say I'm depressing. I'm not,

I don't think. I have a good sense
of humor. I laugh at hot air
balloons drifting over my pancakes.
Don't you? I doubt
that my teacher, Mrs. Grinmore,
reads what we write. On page four
I wrote f___ three hundred times.

I get an A. Maybe Hardy
would love page four,
his characters like markers
stashed in books that end up
in garage sales or under beds.

STEVE BURNING

Sophomore year in high school
I'm a mess, crave sex

with a man. Dear Jesus
please make me want to marry
a girl. In your Name. Amen.

Kenny Rogers and the First Edition's
"Something's Burning" hitbound
on WCFL. Kenny sings
how love is something burning.
My friends and I talk music constantly.
Alan says the song's too *passionate*.
Pastor Frank wouldn't like me

humming along. When mom
burns the chocolate pudding,
I picture Gino,
a seat behind me in geometry,

ask to lick the spoon.

STEVE'S SECRETS

Some fill their pockets
with gum, apples, erasers.
Not me. Mine hold secrets.

I'm often asked why do
my suits bulge?

I'm secret-bumpy. Sometimes
I reach into a pocket and pull out
a surprise. At the fancy dinner

with the gummy bear butler,
I expose a juicy one, expect
to be sent home unfed--
instead, a woman beside me
says my, how interesting.
A guy beside her says he
has one just like it. Maybe

I should empty my pockets.
No doubt, I'd feel lighter.
Nah, anything that I could
pull out of my pockets,
that's easy. Secrets
I can't admit to myself--
no pocket is deep enough

to hold those that slip
into creases, weave
a lint cocoon,
wait their time.

OUT FROM UNDER

Teachers, blank as unsigned hallway passes.
Steve searches for a crack so thin under the basketball court that he'll slip away, his body light as a note.

Steve's dad watches Cubs baseball, Bears football, and Bulls basketball.

Eighth grade gymnastics. Words like "parallel bars" mean torture. Or the rope. Why not just use a ladder? At least in gymnastics he even halfway enjoys leaping on the trampoline, sensing that maybe he could jump high enough to float out of junior high forever. Gravity, a stubborn hag, always call him back.

In high school gym Steve finds his thin crack under the court. While mastering the art of invisibility.

A college sophomore, Steve goes home for Thanksgiving. The turkey tastes like dirty tires. Sometimes

> the world cracks. For good. The sound deepens.
> You emerge.

THE BARGAIN

His grandfather called Steve #1,
a perfect boy. Perfection
is poison but it can soothe.
The family told him to lead
mourners to the casket.
He wanted wings to escape.
The black suit prevented flight,
Reynolds Funeral Home a cage.

At home, he fell asleep for
twelve hours, woke as a parrot,
uncaged in the living room.
He didn't expect to become

a bird. One day you're
wearing black and the next
you're green—which feels better
than the clunk of human bones,
a rolodex brain overstuffed
with repeating images.

Feathers landed in his corn flakes.
He perched on sorrow,
bargained with the window
to make it open just once.

A GRIEF

Steve's parents told him
"Be good." So good,

he became
an orange

in the back
of the fridge,

softening,
rotting out,

a shapeless
mess under

a wet rag,
a grief

nobody
admits to.

TRACING PAPER

Rain plunks a tinny
piano. Thunder, an amplified

heartbeat. Steve goes out,
lets summer swerve

down his skin, won't go in
till he's soaked, sits

by the window watching
the sky's gray tracing

paper take night's first
pencil prick.

STUDIO APARTMENT

Turning on the stairs,
he sees a shadow. A fist
bangs against a wooden door.
His dreams fill with falling teeth,
cups, severed heads.
Bricks lean against him.
He prays to 8 locks,
lights incense to ease
the garbage stink.

One floor above, a body
walks all night,
a creaking ghost. Sometimes
around two a.m.
lobby doorbells zing. Shrill
laughter. The cell phone
would ring if it could. Breath
hangs between wires, fog.

I am here.
I am here.

He takes the moon down
closing a curtain.

STEVE'S FOREIGN LANGUAGE

The moon teaches foreign language
to anyone who cares to listen.
Tonight its light
is Swahili. Tomorrow, who knows?
Probably Uranusian--oh,
lovely the language the moon knows
by heart, lovely
each syllabic elm, leaves
accenting bark and branch.

Join me in class.
We'll listen carefully,
since the moon encourages
a love note exchanged
between strangers,

never allows
men to wear suits
or women to wear girdles.
I'm going naked--are you coming?

I'd love lying with you under a maple
looking up at our teacher
presenting comet dialects.

STORY OF A GARDEN

The soul buries herself

in the deepest brain folds,
spreads herself so thin
that she can't be detected
in breath, prefers dark

basements, caverns. Bats
hang near souls in caves--
if we think we *possess*
our souls, bats know better.

One place reveals the soul:
a garden.

Take Steve. Messy guy,
sloppy style, can't match
his clothes, craggy beard.

In his garden yellows brag
into blues brag into magentas.
Leaves leak over circles
and twining trapezoids.
Blossoms scrounge
around stem tops.

His soul dis-
appears in a crack
at the edge
of a bud--

visible, alert.

BY HAND

I break up
grass clumps. Tools--

the craven claw,
the poker-faced trowel,
the ravenous shovel,
a sad lot taking on
clay balls, stones.
My finger roots push

deep into dirt and muck.
In the shower
water breaks my cocoon:

A moth, I emerge,
find the first bud
to balance on.

EMPTY TREE

AFRAID TO TELL

Steve's afraid to tell
his doctor that he's
gay, afraid his insurance

company will find out,
afraid his boss will find
out, afraid if he charges

a book in a gay bookstore
it will be recorded
and detected in a distant room,

afraid to get an AIDS test,
afraid not to,
afraid he's under

too much stress,
might have a stroke,
eyes lifeless in a wheelchair.

STEVE STEW

Sadness widens until it's big
as my shadow. Nothing outruns
or overtakes it. Black and blue
with self-pity, either I pig
out on pizza, shop, listen to
Brenda and the Tabulations,
or just sit at the front window
watching winter winds snarl at snow.

When the phone rings, I don't answer.
If I hear someone press my bell,
I pretend I'm not home and wait
until they go. I'm vinegar
saturated meat, a bad smell
sinking in as I marinate.

STEVE'S FRIDGE LOOKED INTO

I hold the work party
this year. Someone opens
my fridge, sees TV dinners,
gin and jelly—
a real bachelor's fridge, she says.

A bachelor? Just because

I've loved a man for almost
twenty-five years, will I always
be a bachelor,
un-married, the guy
without enough fruit
in his bins? Their
wedding rings won't stop
barking! I'm the hum

of a fridge, a dirty counter,
not the man
who loves a man
who loves a man.

STEVE COMPLEX

Goodbye phone: I'm put on
hold with horrible music
after I press a key—
the key

is simplicity. My life is
like a grocery bag—
the bottom breaks,
cans roll across the parking lot.

I disappear into machines,
or worse, they disappear
into me. Maybe

I'll disconnect from everything,
even people, listening for
a gloxinia's purple and white
heartbeat—the bud

asks nothing but to startle
a stem.

BROWN CORDS

His first time in
a gay bar, Steve wore
brown cords, a pack
of Newports in his pocket.
Some guy asked him to dance
to "Dancing Queen"
and put his hand on Steve's ass—
part of him wanted to say
stop that,
part of him wanted to say
more please.

After the song ended,
the stranger slipped away
into other dancers.

Steve ordered a gin and tonic,
more at ease
but ready to go.

LEFT-HANDED MONKEY WRENCH

A left-handed monkey
wrench rusts in Steve's garage.
His uncle said his grandfather
used it to kill a neighbor. Steve

wonders how long before
someone monkeys around
with him, smells oil and gasoline
on rags. Bushels of leaves

hug tires. He pictures frost
bolting his deep
blue eyes.

SNAPSHOT

Steve slips it in
a stack of random pictures
he took from his mother's dresser
after she died. A bomb,

it could explode while he sleeps,
yet he could forget it's there.

Several years later,
while sorting through them,
detonation. Family.
Some remember what they want,
shove the rest into
a glove compartment.

Sell the car.
It never happened.

SMILE

When he's in trouble,
he smiles, is considered
"easy to work with," hides

the smile in his briefcase
at 5 p.m., locks it in
a strongbox at home,

scared it might get out
while he's sleeping,
wind around his throat,

do him in.

STEVE'S LOBSTERS

A scorching July morning.
Steve in the Safe-Shop
holds sweaty coupons.
Just before swinging his cart
toward canned carrots, he
glimpses lobsters in a tank.

As human tongs pull things
from shelves, fluorescent
lighting makes shoppers look
like bodies in Webster's
Funeral Home. Steve wants

to pull each lobster into
the safety of his arms,
despite cutting claws.
This is not the Maine coast.
This is Parkersburg,
West Virginia, where sea

creatures swim into pots. He
pulls away from the doomed,
heads to fast checkout,
grabs a *Globe* which says
dieting Jesus will soon return.
God on talk shows with psychics
to the stars.

In The Safe-Shop's huge tank,
he's an aging lobster--

the scanner's red eye
squints on his purchases,
his car the boiling water
he drops into.

I-95

As he drives, a tornado warning,
sky like the bruise he got
from being pushed down the stairs
in eighth grade. He sees
a billboard: LEADERSHIP MATTERS.

Steve's never been a leader,
prefers the end of lines
even if he has to wait.

The one high school class he failed,
Speech. He sweated and stammered,
looked away from his listeners,
sat down, a stubby pencil eraser.

The tornado must be near.
Pelting rain, cars pulling off to the side.
He keeps going, perhaps into
wind's jaw, Or maybe,

in a few more minutes,
a calm dusk opening its lily bud
across the city skyline.

REALLY?

Bar chitter-chatter
turns to gay issues.
Steve doesn't bring any up,
the only queer there.
Bring them up
and he's accused
of wanting to be
a full human being,
not 75% of one
the way Jefferson thought
about his slaves
even as he fucked one
who couldn't refuse him.
A good liberal
mentioned gays,
thought things were much
better now.

When Steve said
there isn't
a single hour
when I am free
of the knowledge
that I could be assaulted,
my house vandalized,
my lover killed,

the good liberal said,
"Really?"

The conversation shifted to baseball deals. Steve forgets what was said.

OVERHEARD

The mailbox snaps at the iris.

*What's the matter? You think it's easy
being a mailbox? Open wide. Eat.
Then our owner pulls it all out,
leaves me empty. Rain. I rust.
Last year a huge truck clipped me.
I went flying. I'm dented for good.*

The iris sniffs.

*Troubles? You want troubles?
I bloom for maybe two weeks tops.
For fifty weeks I'm boring.
Some years I open only to have
wind and rain tether me
to the ground.*

Steve thinks he should break this up,
let the road referee their grief--

after it finishes moaning
about all the clunky vehicles
that it must hold up,
tire marks, winter salt,
and cigarettes searing
tar skin.

ODORS FROM OTHER WINDOWS

Come, night,
play your piano on my roof
when a chrysanthemum slides

panel-petals open. I sniff
the spice-earth aroma in
a black dune

of moonless night:
a few flowers blot out
odors from other windows.

SWIMMER STEVE

I keep my head
just above the water,
a floating beach ball.

My astronomer friend Lek
says Mars' north polar
ice cap has water--that would
be rough swimming.
Wait long enough

and blue becomes red, truth
wags a new tail. I picture me
breaststroking under
a sky with two moons,
like I'm seeing double

through fogged goggles. Phobos
And Deimos, lifeguards,
handsome ones at that.

STEVE AFTER JOGGING

Eighth grade surges back—

I've drunk milk from a carton,
and am now on the playground,
keeping myself on the opposite end from .
Roger Stretsky--kids call him Papa--
a blond snot who sneaks up on boys
and with his index finger hooks
their balls through their pants. This is

a riot, I guess. Awkward in gym,
uncoordinated, dribble so badly
the ball wobbles to bleachers.
Thirty years later

I picture Papa tossed in a dumpster,
hear him scream "Help me!"
I turn on the ignition, drive off.

STEVE OUT FOR A WALK

Oh, the TV blue
haze in dark picture windows--ten houses,

each glowing. Cut
people open,
DVDs roll out. A guy I know

actually cried when he heard
Happy Days got cancelled.
The 80s. Cut me open,

and weird angels would pop
out of my veins, spurt
from arteries. Locks

copulate with keys. Scared,
we install "security" systems.
One by one TVs drizzle off.

Dreams come up drainpipes,
seep into eyes. Even in sleep,
channel surfing.

STEVE AND THE EMPTY TREE

Make me a leafless
tree.

Sparrows visit my branches,
sing, fly. Winter
gets nasty, but how sweet
to let everything go,

to stand before
a falling flake,
an acrobat leaping
from a cloud,
resembling only itself,

wind carrying it
through me.

STEVE BARKING AT THE MOON

Dusk. The moon rows
toward shore, passes
trees leafing. Grass
greening my ankle.

Signs appear—
the crow
is really an owl.
A dog barks.

I have my sign,
bones of a shadow.
A ragged moan,
then nothing.

STEVE PAINTING

When I was ten, my mother
asked Pastor Clack could
she wear makeup? Yes,
he said, because old barns
need fresh paint. I'm

painting my porch
picturing mom as a barn.
My friend Shirley loves lipstick.
I lightly spritz on cologne--
are Shirley and I
old barns? I paint and paint,

fingers whitening, can't keep
my brush from swiping
the floor. In the locker room
men primp, spray, shave,
and comb. Seventy years:

if I am an old barn,
Death will raze me,
give my bones
a more natural look.

STEVE READY

His childhood minister said
to *keep ready*--Jesus might be
coming, no time to *get ready*,
so he kept ready as a hydrant,
kept checking the sky to see
if it could be parting
the way a technicolor sea
parted for Heston. When

he saw how four
o'clocks
in the raised bed don't keep
ready, he quit keeping ready too--
they sprout, grow,
expose elegant blossoms,

go poof. No sky
parts for them. They provide
just the right colors
for any emergency--

how could they be
more perfect?

STEVE READS *HUCK FINN*

Even on weekends he gets up
at 6:00, each day like curtains
that no breeze moves, no
feisty current, just streets
piling up on each other
like gear in an overstuffed

tackle box. His bank job
requires a tie which requires
a desire to hang from a ceiling
until someone cuts him down.
Huck owned little
but had adventure—

the river could veer this way
or that, strangers could rise
like bubbles, wherever the raft
would land you could end up
eating fried chicken or running

for your life. Instead of a raft,
a mall sucks Steve in. He buys
nothing, can't face his home
TV's seductive demand
to be watched.

STEVE STARRING IN BERGMAN'S *Cries and Whispers*

He didn't cast me. I appear anyway,
play a secret sister named Agnetha.
Barely photographed, getting none
of Nykvist's loving closeups, I slide

in the background, polish silverware,
dust clocks, hum. Ingmar can't
understand why I keep interfering
with his shots. *Get him out of here,*
he says—bulbous Swedish dresses
disguise me. My beard a veil.
Credits don't list me. The Academy notes
my performance. I'm nominated
in Best Invisible Actor Or Actress

in a Foreign Film. Ingmar returns to Faro,
Liv returns to America to choose
her next project, and I return
to the Acme, drop six grapefruits
in my basket, then speed home
to read fan mail that never comes.

WHAT STEVE DID ON HIS SUMMER VACATION

In high school, Erich and I said
that someday we'd take
the greatest vacation

ever. I suggested Charon,
but he asked why not dash over
to a more private moon like Kerberos?
Dorothy had ruby slippers to work
magic. All we'll pack is imagination.
It gets you everywhere,
no jacket required. We'll speed

past Neptune and soon Kerberos
will show us frozen fig trees,
a dark little place despite
a movie-star sun posing for pictures
that get plastered all over
the Kuiper Belt. We'll forget

about Earth steeped in wars and religion,
a darker world,
ruined.

DRY SPELL

Steve hates bars,
but Woody's is where
the action is, he hears, so
he squeezes into black
jeans, a cranberry red shirt,
a pack of Newport Light 100s
in his pocket. He orders

a very dry martini,
sits on a stool next to nobody,
thinks about how Paul Henreid
lit Bette Davis's cigarette.
Puffing hard, he walks around,
returns to his still-empty stool.
A man who says he runs
a dirty bookstore buys him
a drink, asks would he like
to come back to his place—
hardly Paul Henreid.

Steve slips out the door jammed
with pretty boys,
back to two cats by the window,
a pink fridge humming off-key
beside a stinking sink.

THE JOKE

Having survived high
school gym, enduring
taunts and slaps (oh,
sweet teamwork), I
thought I'd never risk
a locker room again.

Well, here I am,

though now many
of the guys are over 65.
Some I like, those who
seem like painted daisies,
ready for their second
blooming of the season.

Others have faces
like closed accounts.

I cover the truth like its
my towel.

They joke about fags,
can't imagine one could
be showering beside them.

I'm supposed to be
the joke,
not the reality.

TURBULENCE

30,000 feet up Steve closes his eyes,
muffles a scream. Despite bumps
servers take his order. The pilot
announces yet another
bad patch—
if armrests were skin,
he'd leave scars.

Safe at last on the runway,
he remembers the Pope kissing
ground upon landing.
What turbulence does he feel?

Walking into the real world
again, worse turbulence—
strangers bump
in bright hallways, run,
stop short, run again,
pilot death at the controls.

LATELY

STEVE THIS MORNING

That turquoise,

if only I could wear it so boldly.
The morning

glory took four months to climb
up our rusted flagpole
which flies a flag of allegiance
only to budding tendrils.

Much of a vine's life is getting
in a position to make
flowering possible.
In that way, we're similar.

I don't need a flagpole
but I do need love--
I turn my head to the sky.
Before I know it, I'm open,
morning in me,
if only for a few hours.

MORNING COFFEE AND EVENING STENCH

Today God wears his favorite
fishnet stockings and makes the sun
whirr. I turn on

the coffee maker. Everyone into
making things and still
not even seven a.m. As hour

weeds out hour, I retain
my good mood, partly because
WFJL plays The Balloon Farm's

"A Question of Temperature"
which I haven't heard since '68.
Evening—I plop on the porch glider,

like that word, *glider*,
it sounds so boogity and boffo,
until an awful stench

rolls in, something between
cat piss and burnt motor oil.
Oh, how quickly a day can

turn into a needle
with disease shot straight
in the arm! It stinks,

but garbage men will come
tomorrow, God will gas up
another sun. I'll drink

more Maxwell House, dawn's
red canes poking out

STEVE AND THE BURGLAR

He broke in
after I had gone to bed.

I never heard the door open. He stood
in my hall. I keep a gun by my nightstand,
nothing fancy. I shot him,

right through his heart. Instead of blood,
flowers quickly shot out of his chest,
orchids and clivias. He dropped
on my balcony. I put a blanket around him
and watered him. He apologized.
I went back to bed. In the morning

he thanked me for a great evening.
Perhaps he'll return
in full bloom.

STEVE IN PURGATORY

Not Catholic, but
I'm here anyway with
Abe Lincoln and Georgia O'Keeffe,
Dante and Lucille Ball. Nobody

suffers but nobody's happy. We miss
Earth's extremes. This is like eating
in a diner which only serves
great oatmeal. I must work through

many sins, the big one,
arrogance. I thought if people
believed as I did, all would be well,
believed I had the facts

while others put on acts. Now
I pretend oatmeal
is French onion soup. No flowers here--too extreme,

too lovely. We live in a huge burb,
each house the same,
hunt for a way to be different,
70 degrees for centuries.

STEVE IN PARADISE

I couldn't tell much
difference between Hell
and Earth except
the circles were more clear,
the Devil more visible.

Purgatory reminded me of Aunt Rita
telling us for the millionth time
how her maid who stole her
black dress was still
wearing it in jail. The sign

says this is Paradise,
a kind of ongoing Provincetown
at time's sandy tip.
Anyone's welcome provided
they're charming. That alone
makes Paradise stranger
than the sad little world I left--

here colors whirl in a mad mash,
petals pop open like Betty Boop's
eyes. Many who died disgraced
on the sad little world
relax on porches
shaded by trees even in winter.

We walk, greet each other,
read good books. God runs
down any street, the best
ostrich in town.

STEVE DISAPPEARING

He works out
in the morning
mostly him
and older guys
whose fallen
chests comfort
him: *I am
not that yet.*
After showering,
steam fades him in
and out of the mirror.
He heads to his locker,
changes, feels his skin
damp, disappearing.

STEVE CUTS

twenty fat branches
from a purple lilac bush,
puts them in vases—hopes
his grandparents will visit
in his sleep.

Ann put lilac-stuffed
vases in each room.
Earl never noticed,
was Bears football,
Sunday car repairs.
Strangers bought their house
when they died. Twenty years--

flowers, firm for a few days,
droop on the table.

STEVE AND CHILDREN

From across the street a small
boy asks Steve,

Mister, do you like children?

Sure, Steve says,
knowing he sounds false.
With some kids he stays
inside when kids play outside—
childhood, a loft

he got locked in,
something moving in the dark.

STEVE IN THE ORCHARD

October: I breathe in
rotting fruit, flatten rinds
under my shoes. Only

cemeteries bring me such
peace: names, apples just
let go. Many trees here

will outlive me, decades
caught in gnarls, years line
old nests. So much to listen to:

wind, crickets, sparrows,
a car's whoosh. Apple trees,
darkened houses, no fruit shining.

A stranger might think I look
like I'm hunting for an address
on a strange street—

I watch leaves meet the ground,
a friend who takes them in,
who turns no one away.

EARLY

I'm just getting out of the shower
when Tony arrives, always at least
ten minutes early. He's said don't blame him--

his mother was the same way, took him to school
and he'd always be first in line. I toss on
sweats and a threadbare red tee,

dash downstairs to let him in.
He whines, "Steve, what took you so long?"
Shampoo bubbles pop in my hair. I tell him

"I'll only be a minute." He clicks to
the weather channel, shouts out
Angolan temps. We're going

to Ruby Tuesdays, only half a mile away. Not all early birds
annoy. This morning I noticed
four oriental poppies have pushed up,

six weeks early. Tony sniffs.
A flower's a flower to him. He likes NASCAR
and drag queens. Go figure.

AFRICAN VIOLET STEVE

He sees beauty in few places,
but when he does, he stops,
or to him, Earth slows its orbit,
the moon releases the tides,

briefly. Beauty breaks down.
He's now on his twenty-fifth
african violet, having killed each one:
too little water, too little heat,
not the right light, oh,
it's terrible to love something
and get it wrong, green pads
blackening. An optimist,

he tries again. His dad grows one
that's seven years old—
never out of bloom,
a man who prefers NASCAR to gardens.
His friend Sue tries to help--
several thrive in her apartment.
Steve wants the world to stop

turning, even once, time
descending on a bud just opened,
lavender flowers, small and perfect,
and likely not to last.

STEVE LOOKS AT CLOUDS

out
    in drag today
clouds change
                fast
imitate
       no one
               white scarves
flung just above
           treetops
     touch of gray
surprise
                moving
    all
of us
    in the neighborhood
to come
           out
     admire
such grace

THE NIGHT HAS 1007 EYES

Millie says, "Oh man, here you go again, you're like a zebra that died in a zoo."

What can I say? I am a croaked zebra and I can't lighten up. Life is unyieldingly terrible. Zoo zebras have it better, actually. They get fed on time. Most of the world doesn't.

But most of the world can't fly and I can. I'm like Sister Bertrille in *The Flying Nun* only I weigh 220 pounds, and I'm gay. I don't know if Sister was a lesbian. There were rumors. About Carlos too.

When I fly, I can't go too high. I'd like to make the moon someday, but I settle for penthouses. I'm a bit of a Peeping Tom. Though my name is Steve.

I've learned a few things airborne. It's no better up here than down there, but at least it's not down where teachers give kids writing lessons, the ink always red, and after the lesson they have to drink it so they die.

Millie also says, "I get high from living."

Huh? I get high from being separated even for a few moments from the disaster called mankind.

Wait a second—don't think I was always a crab. I was a cheerful boy, a yes ma'am yes sir kind of kid. I got blue ribbons for deportment, held my farts in even when they would have made other kids laugh.

I fell in love. It never worked out. Now I don't bother with it. I fly over love's graveyard and believe in no resurrection.

I had a job. Ten jobs. All were snakes swimming in cold chicken noodle soup. Quitting became a talent. When bill collectors come after me, I fly. Go ahead, take whatever I have. I can live on a balcony or a branch.

I was raised to be a good Baptist. Jesus and I swam in the

springs of living water. We'd have races and of course he always won so I got bored with him.

Jesus: "But you have to love me--I insist."

Me: "You're all about you. Even on the cross you had it planned out that you'd collect on the worship. I've gotta fly. Bye."

One thing scientists haven't figured out yet—the night has 1007 eyes. We're being watched, not by God, but by the night. Stars aren't the eyes. They're hidden. They're seeing you now. What are you doing? It will come out—everything will.

I fly into a pupil, recline in a blink. Another war breaks out. An eye fills with tears. Impotent tears. The sun rises. Night goes blind in one eye, but the others keep watching.

DOLLY PARTON

Steve says that Dolly sings his life. He's
hardly from Tennessee, grew up
in northern Illinois, childhood's speedy water

rushing away. When he's sad
he opens his mouth
and a country song comes out,
almost like opening a music box. Tonight

Dolly sings that her life
is like a bargain store.
Under the awning of a guitar chord,
Steve stays dry as rain pelts down.
The sun stumbles out, drunk,

gold coins
falling all over the county.

STEVE'S OPEN FLOWER

Steve can't stay still--
that's why he flunks out,
can't hold a job.

In a big cemetery, he shakes
imaginary hands of dead strangers,
kicks leaves off plots, lies down
to hear the dead speak
through grass. Even in winter,
he lies down, a snowflake's breath
on his neck, snow out-

lining his shape. Up again,
he walks back to his car,
drives home, wind at his window
a stranger asking him to dance—
they do, in silence, out in

the open flower of death.

BLUE TRAIN

A blue train has no depots,
circles and circles, never stops.
The engineer swerves,
sleeps. At first I thought

my destination was near.
After a week I forget
where I was in such a hurry
to get to. The conductor
tears my ticket

to confetti, has been riding
this line all his life,
claims some folks are born,
die and are reborn on this trip.

His words fly to the window,
a glass coffin.

STEVE'S FLASHLIGHT

I ask Steve if he thinks that the world
is more inclined to light
or darkness. That's easy, he says,
darkness. I offer him a flashlight
to help him see in his moon-free
evening of a life. He refuses it,
says that the batteries will go.
Then where will he be?

He's like a chalkboard,
the word NO written 500 times
across it. I must admit
that more than half the time
he's proven right. I say *Look,
here comes the sun.* He says sooner
or later it will swell and devour us.
It's true. I saw it on *Cosmos*.

Perhaps he sees some sweetness
in the approaching ruin.
He's tasted it, gets out of bed
seizing the day, a beautiful day,
finches bounding down to coneflowers,
day that quickly end.

STEVE FLICKERS

At the concert darkness
covers us, a heavy coat.
We flick lighters,
make a tender glow.

We'll try to find our way home,
headachy, high, the roads,
tough crossword puzzles.
Something always right
on the tongue's tip
keeps slipping away, the puzzle
not quite finished.

When I die forget candles,
lighters, or matches,
not even songs. Dump me
around some roses. Maybe

I'll improve your spring,
the least I can do—
and the most.

STEVE LATELY

Lately I've had such
colorful dreams--my brain glints,
    a rolex in the sun
  for sale on Christopher Street—
      my sleep more lively
than my waking: I'm quickly
                            be-
  coming several people: minstrel,
  criminal, barber, waitress, drag
    queen--my self
               says: Everyone's Welcome.
  The more
  I divide
  the more I am one, light on
  a pigeon's feathers--so many
  of me to give away, the way

  a mad rich man stands on top
  of a skyscraper and dumps money
  on heads passing below. I know
    why he looks joyous--this
getting rid of, emptying the self,
              putting it
in another's arms, on a busy street.

ABOUT THE AUTHOR

Kenneth Pobo has eleven books and thirty chapbooks published. *Your Place Or Mine* is winner of the Alabama Poetry Society's annual contest. His work has appeared in or is forthcoming in *North Dakota Quarterly, Nimrod, Mudfish, Atlanta Review, Hawaii Review, Amsterdam Review, The Queer South Anthology,* and elsewhere.

facebook.com/kenneth.pobo
twitter.com/Kenpobo

ALSO BY KENNETH POBO

BOOKS

Wingbuds, www.cyberwit.net, Allahabad, India, 2019.

Dindi Expecting Snow, Seattle, WA: Duck Lake Books, 2019.

The Antlantis Hit Parade, Auburn, NY: Clare Songbirds Press, 2019.

Loplop in a Red City, Richmond, VA: Circling Rivers, 2017.

Booking Rooms in the Kuiper Belt, Windsor: Urban Farmhouse Press, 2015.

Bend of Quiet. San Francisco: Blue Light Press, 2015.

Glass Garden. Cincinatti: WordTech Press, 2008.

Introductions. Atlanta: Pearl's Book'Em Publisher, 2003.

Ordering: A Season in My Garden. Higganum, CT: Higganum Hills Books, 2001.

Musings from the Porchlit Sea. Boston: Branden Books, 1979.

Opening. Recto Y Versos (forthcoming).

CHAPBOOKS

Your Place Or Mine. Brierfield, AL: The Alabama State Poetry Society, 2020.

Book of Micah. Philadelphia, PA: Moonstone Arts, 2020.

Snowflake. Local Gems Poetry Press, 2019.

Threads, Yavanika Press, https://yavanikapress.wixsite.com. 2019.

Dust And Chrysanthemums, Grey Borders Books, Niagara Falls, ON, 2017.

Calligraphy With Ball, Farmington, ME: Encircle Press, 2017.

Highway Rain, Masillon, OH: Poet's Haven Press, 2015.

When The Light Turns Green, West Chester, PA: Spruce Alley Press, 2014.

Placemats, Gloucester, MA: Eastern Point Press, 2013.

Save My Place, Georgetown, KY: Finishing Line Press, 2012.

Ice And Gaywings, Montreal, QC: Phoenicia Press, 2011.

Tiny Torn Maps, Deadly Chaps, 2011.

Contralto Crows, Loveland, CO: Green Fuse Press, 2011.

Closer Walks, Thunderclap Press, 2011.

Tea on Burning Glass, Calumet, MI: Tandava Poetry Press, 2010.

Fitting Parts, Philistine Press, http://www.philistinepress.com, 2010.

Trina and the Sky, Charlotte, NC: Main Street Rag Press, 2009.

Something To Be Said, Flutter Press, http://www.flutterpress.webs.com.

Crazy Cakes. Scars Publications, http://scars.tv, June 2008.

Postcards from America. Origami Condom (Tamafyhr Mountain Press), 2004: www.origamiconsom.org/chapbooks.html.

Kenneth Pobo's Greatest Hits. Johnstown, OH: Pudding House Press, 2002.

Open To All. Amherst, NY: 2River View, 2000.

Cicadas And Apple Trees. Aiken, SC: Palanquin Press, 1998.

A Barbaric Yawp on the Rocks. New Hope, PA: Alpha Beat Press, 1996.

Ravens and Bad Bananas. Ann Arbor, MI: Osric Publishing, 1995.

Yes: Irises. Canton, CT: Singular Speech Press, 1999.

Ferns On Fire. Troy, ME: Nightshade Press, 1991.

A Pause Inside Dusk. Stevens Point, WI: Song Press, 1986.

Evergreen. Boulder, CO: Bragdon Books, 1985.

Billions of Lit Cigarettes. Doylestown, PA: Raw Dog Press, 1981.

www.ingramcontent.com/pod-product-compliance
Lightning Source LLC
Chambersburg PA
CBHW030001110526
44587CB00012BA/1158